Now, over 300
types of birds
have made the
Rift Valley Lakes
their home.

ሐይቆቹ ከ300 በላይ
የወፍ ዝርያ ዓይነቶችን
አስጠልለው ይዘዋል።

They eat from the lakes

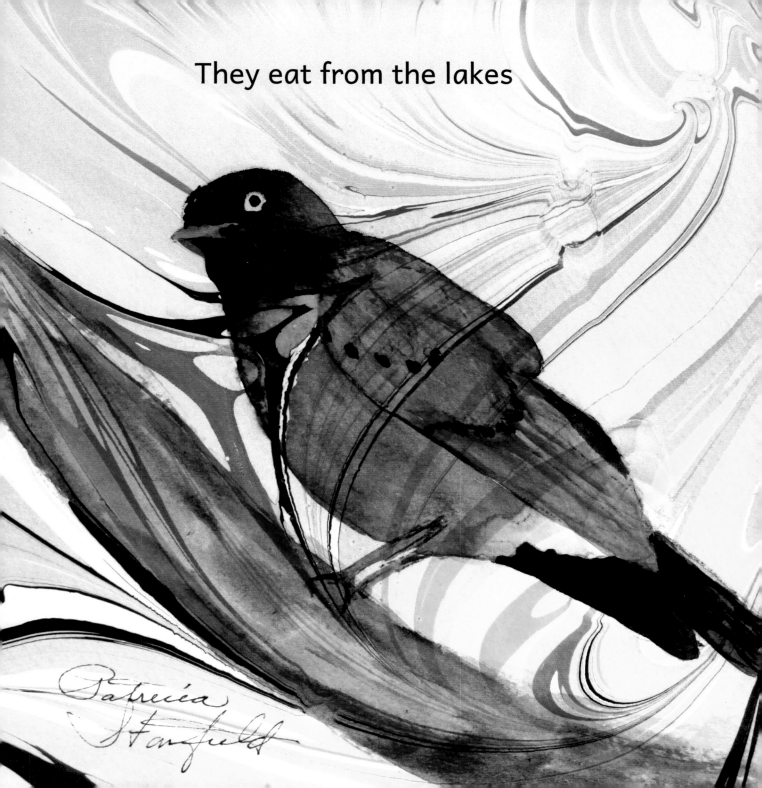

Thank you to the generous team who gave their time
and talents to make this book possible:

Author
Noh Goering

Illustrators
Rebekah Mitsein and Lee Baughman's watercolor students at
Clark College Community and Economic Development, Vancouver, WA

Creative directors
Caroline Kurtz, Jane Kurtz and Kenny Rasmussen

Translator
Amlaku B. Eshetie

Designer
Beth Crow

Ready Set Go Books, an Open Hearts Big Dreams Project

Special thanks to Ethiopia Reads donors and staff for believing in this project and helping get it started-- and for arranging printing, distribution, and training in Ethiopia.

ISBN: 979-8563267367
Library of Congress Control Number: 2020922431

Republished: 11/11/20

የታላቁ ስምጥ ሸለቆ ሐይቆች

The Great Rift Valley Lakes

English and Amharic

Eighteen million years
ago the ground in Africa
began to crack open.

ከብዙ ፤ ብዙ ዓመታት በፊት
የአፍሪካ መሬት መሰንጠቅ
ጀመረ።

This is how the Rift Valley was made.

ስምጥ ሸለቆው የተፈጠረው እንደዚህ ነበር።

Ethiopia ended up with a chain
of 7 Rift Valley Lakes.

ኢትዮጵያ የ7 ሐይቆች
ሰንሰለት እንዲኖራት
አደረገ።

They drink and take
baths in the lakes.

ከሐይቁ ይጠጣሉ፤
ይታጠባሉ።

They also make their
nests by the lakes.

ጎጇዎቻቸውን በሐይቆቹ
አጠገብ ይሠራሉ።

Pink flamingos fly over the lakes like pink clouds.

ሮዝ ፍላሚንጎዎች በሐይቁ ላይ በሮዝ ዳመናዎች ውስጥ ይበርራሉ።

Twenty-three types of birds can be found only in Ethiopia and nowhere else.

ሃያ ሶስት ዓይነት የወፍ ዝርያ ዓይነቶችን በኢትዮጵያ ውስጥ ብቻ የሚገኙ ናቸው።

Birds aren't the only animals that live near the lakes.

በሐይቁ አጠገብ የሚኖሩ እንስሳት ወፎች ብቻ አይደሉም።

At Nechisar National Park, 70 types of mammals live by the lakeshores.

በነጭ ሳር ብሔራዊ ፓርክ 70 ዓይነት አጥቢ እንስሳት በሐይቆቹ ዙሪያ ይኖራሉ።

Oryx sprint in the grass up to 37 miles per hour (60 kilometers per hour).

የበረሃ ፍየል በሳሩ ውስጥ በሰዓት እስከ 37 ማይል ወይም 60 ኪሎሜትር መሮጥ ይችላል።

Zebras munch the grass.

ዜብራዎች ዛሩን ይግጣሉ።

CarolRose

They sleep standing up.

በቁማቸው እንቅልፋቸውን ያንቀላፉሉ።

Baboons carry their babies by giving them piggyback rides.

ዝንጀሮዎች ልጆቻቸውን በጀርባቸው አዝለው ይሮጣሉ።

People live by the lakes too.

ሰዎችም እንደወፎችና እንስሳት ሁሉ በሐይቆች ዙሪያ ይኖራሉ።

People herd their cows and camels beside the lakes.

ላሞችና ግመሎችን በሐይቁ ዙሪያ ያሰማራሉ።

Near Lake Shala, people have even started an ostrich farm.

ሻላ ሐይቅ አጠገብም
የሰጎን ፓርክም
አቋቁመዋል፤

The lakes are a magical place
to visit or live.

ሐይቆች ለመኖብነትም ሆነ
ለመኖርም ምትሃታዊ ወይም
አስደናቂ ቦታዎች ናቸው።

About The Story

People come from many countries to visit some of the Rift Valley Lakes. The Nechisar National Park has a strip of land called the 'Bridge of God' which separates 2 lakes. The park protects the white grass plains. There are 15 endemic butterflies, and 8 endemic dragonflies which can be seen on the lakeshores. In Lake Shala there are nine islands with pelicans on all of them. One island is even called Pelican Island.

Thank you to Vast Ethiopia Tours for some of the information in this book.
http://www.vastethiopiatours.com/

About The Author

Noh Goering was born in Kansas, but he traveled to Ethiopia to meet his mother's family when he was only a year old. When he was eleven, he was visiting Jane Kurtz (his grandmother) in Portland and saw the art that the Clark College painters created to show the land and people and animals around Rift Valley lakes in Ethiopia. He chose which paintings he wanted to include and did research so he could write an informational story.

Noh attends middle school in Orlando, Florida. In his spare time, he likes to play soccer.

About The Illustrators

The art for this book was created by painters attending Lee Baughman's morning and evening Watercolor classes at Clark College Continuing Education in Vancouver, Washington. The men and women who donated their time and talent were delighted to participate in a project that is furthering literacy, since many of them are current or former educators themselves. Many of the artists experimented with new marbling and layering techniques while creating these paintings. Several researched the specific animal they painted, and excitedly shared their new knowledge with their fellow artists.

Margaret Webb is an artist from Vancouver, Washington who has been drawing and painting animals, wildlife, landscapes and still-life since she was young. She says, "It was a pleasure donating the 'Ethiopian Mother & Child' original watercolor painting for this project. My hope is this book will be an educational tool that may inspire a young reader to become an artist or writer sometime in their future. Melikami minyoti. (Best Wishes)"

Rebekah Mitsein has traveled to Ethiopia several times and spent time in Addis Ababa while in college, volunteering at an Ethiopia Reads library for children. She is currently Assistant Professor of English at Boston College, and a specialist on Africa in British texts from 1660-1790. An avid reader from her childhood on, she has helped out where needed with several Ready Set Go Books projects.

As a water media painter Lee Baughman explores the limitless possibilities of watercolor, charcoal and acrylic painting. His interest in exploring the creative process is reflected in his art. Clues to the artist personality and interest can be seen scattered throughout his work. "I paint the things I enjoy having in my life and the things which I want to put into the world," he says.

Lee has been teaching water classes at Clark College's Community Ed. and Mature Learning for 26 years. His classes include watercolor Basics and watercolor 2, as well as two Watercolor, Independent studies.

He is a past president of the Southwest Washington Watercolor Society and has co-led over fifty Art-adventures with Susan Cowan to American, Mexican and European destinations. He has also led numerous workshops such as "Tricks of the Trade" for watercolor with over 40 "tricks" and "Watercolor Batik." He says, "I am excited to believe that by painting a small painting I have the opportunity to touch children on the other side of the planet. The ability to read has enriched my life so much. I am excited to be a part of doing for others."

About Open Hearts Big Dreams

Open Hearts Big Dreams began as a volunteer organization, led by Ellenore Angelidis in Seattle, Washington, to provide sustainable funding and strategic support to Ethiopia Reads, collaborating with Jane Kurtz. OHBD has now grown to be its own nonprofit organization supporting literacy, innovation, and leadership for young people in Ethiopia.

Ellenore Angelidis comes from a family of teachers who believe education is a human right, and opportunity should not depend on your birthplace. And as the adoptive mother of a little girl who was born in Ethiopia and learned to read in the U.S., as well as an aspiring author, she finds the chance to positively impact literacy hugely compelling!

About Ready Set Go Books

Reading has the power to change lives, but many children and adults in Ethiopia cannot read. One reason is that Ethiopia doesn't have enough books in local languages to give people a chance to practice reading. Ready Set Go books wants to close that gap and open a world of ideas and possibilities for kids and their communities.

When you buy a Ready Set Go book, you provide critical funding to create and distribute more books.

Learn more at: http://openheartsbigdreams.org/book-project/

Ready Set Go 10 Books

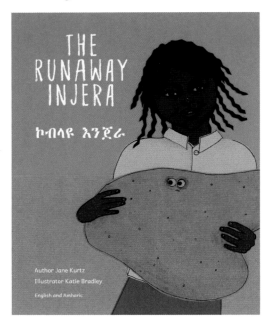

In 2018, Ready Set Go Books decided to experiment by trying a few new books in larger sizes.

Sometimes it was the art that needed a little more room to really shine. Sometimes the story or nonfiction text was a bit more complicated than the short and simple text used in most of our current early reader books.

We called these our "Ready Set Go 10" books as a way to show these ones are bigger and also sometimes have more words on the page. The response has been great so now our Ready Set Go 10 books are a significant number of our titles. We are happy to hear feedback on these new books and on all our books.

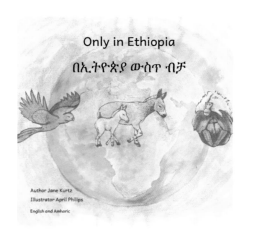

About the Language

Amharic is a Semetic language -- in fact, the world's second-most widely spoken Semetic language, after Arabic. Starting in the 12th century, it became the Ethiopian language that was used in official transactions and schools and became widely spoken all over Ethiopia. It's written with its own characters, over 260 of them. Eritrea and Ethiopia share this alphabet, and they are the only countries in Africa to develop a writing system centuries ago that is still in use today!

About the Translation

Translation is currently being coordinated by a volunteer, Amlaku Bikss Eshetie who has a BA degree in Foreign Languages & Literature, an MA in Teaching English as a Foreign Language, and PhD courses in Applied Linguistics and Communication, all at Addis Ababa University. He taught English from elementary through university levels and is currently a passionate and experienced English-Amharic translator. As a father of three, he also has a special interest in child literacy and development. He can be reached at: khaabba_ils@protonmail.com

Find more Ready Set Go Books on Amazon.com

To view all available titles, search "Ready Set Go Ethiopia" or scan QR code

 Chaos

 Talk Talk Turtle

 The Glory of Gondar

 We Can Stop the Lion

 Not Ready!

 Fifty Lemons

 Count For Me

 Too Brave

 Tell Me What You He

Made in the USA
Monee, IL
23 December 2020